THE

PUNCH

CARTOON
ALBUM

THE

CARTOON ALBUM

150 YEARS OF CLASSIC CARTOONS

EDITED BY AMANDA-JANE DORAN

INTRODUCTION BY MILES KINGTON

A PUNCH BOOK

Published in association with

GRAFTON BOOKS

A Division of the Collins Publishing Group

LONDON GLASGOW
TORONTO SYDNEY AUCKLAND

Grafton Books
A Division of the Collins Publishing Group
8 Grafton Street, London W1X 3LA

Published by Grafton Books 1990

Copyright © Punch Publications Limited 1990

Introduction copyright © Miles Kington 1990

British Library Cataloguing in Publication Data

The Punch cartoon album:
150 years of classic cartoons
1. English humorous cartoons
I. Doran, Amanda-Jane
741.5'942

ISBN 0-246-13645-6

Printed in Great Britain by
Butler & Tanner Ltd, Frome, Somerset

Editor's Note

There have been nearly 500,000 cartoons published in *Punch* over the years, so choosing the best 500 was not particularly easy to do. Fortunately some cartoons chose themselves – there would have been a public outcry if the 'Curate's Egg' or the 'Man Who Paid Off His Overdraft' had been forgotten.

Although styles of drawing have evolved dramatically from the precisely engraved to the free line, the underlying human worries and preoccupations which give cartoonists something to draw about have changed little. In this collection there are Victorian cartoons about manners and love alongside contemporary ones: a rich mélange.

I hope your favourite is here.

My thanks to Chris Burke for his invaluable help with the preparation of this book and whose guffaws kept me going.

Amanda-Jane Doran
Punch Library
London 1990

Introduction *by Miles Kington*

Shortly after I joined the staff of *Punch* in 1968 the Editor, Bernard Hollowood, became ill and retired. I don't think it was anything to do with my arrival. I think it was more to do with years of chagrined realisation that most people thought that Basil Boothroyd was editor of *Punch*. One of the last things that happened under Hollowood's editorship was that *Punch* accepted a cover by George Adamson which showed Mr Punch sitting at an easel in the middle of a stretch of English countryside. Beside him was a book called *How to Paint Like the Great Masters*. And the landscape which Mr Punch was trying to paint was in fact modelled on the great masters, because the Van Gogh trees on the right merged into a Samuel Palmer hillside, then into a Gainsborough or Constable field … To make the landscape itself look like a collaboration between the masters was a brilliant idea. George did it brilliantly and we all thought it was a brilliant cover.

One of the first actions by the new editor, William Davis, was to reject the cover. He didn't understand it. Or, if he did understand it, he didn't think it was funny. Or, if he thought it was funny, he didn't think enough other people would find it was funny. No, let's face it; he didn't understand it. What had happened was that the normal balance of bias against artists at *Punch* had re-established itself. Hollowood had been a writer, as all editors except Kenneth Bird (Fougasse) have been, but he also drew lots of not very good cartoons, and thus had a great respect for people who could draw well – his first act on leaving *Punch* was to write a book about the artist Pont, whereas William Davis would prefer to write a book about money.

Davis had no exaggerated respect for artists. This was normal. He also had no exaggerated respect for writers – I can remember him striding down the corridor shouting: 'The trouble with this magazine is that it's too bloody *literary*!' – and this was rather less normal among editors, and highly welcome. Davis was quite right. The writers have always dominated *Punch* far too much, made their articles too long, over-extended their ideas, persisted in styles of writing which had died out elsewhere (faded light poems, exquisite essays on the day the car broke down). Unfortunately, Davis thought *Punch* was too artistic as well, which was not true and never has been true. The brutal truth about *Punch* – brutal at least to writers – is that it is the cartoons that have established its character, brought it fame and kept it going.

To celebrate 1991, will anyone be bringing out a volume called '150 Years of *Punch* Articles'? I think not. Are there *Punch* writers of a hundred years ago who are still names to be referred to, in the same way that Leech, Keene or du Maurier are referred to ? When phrases go into the English language, like the curate's egg, or 'Bang went saxpence', or Dropping the Pilot, do they come from articles or cartoons?

Could we laugh at *anything* in *Punch* from the last century that wasn't a cartoon?

It's doubtful. Yet the artists have always been second-class citizens, subject to the final decision of the writer. They have been hugely admired, yet not thought in some way quite responsible enough to run the ship, talented yet somehow childlike creatures, like spin-bowlers in cricket, scriptwriters in Hollywood or women in business. Cartoonists working for daily papers today will tell you the same story. Why they don't all rise up one day and slaughter writers, editors and sub-editors in one great revenge massacre, I don't know.

Probably because, like women, they have learnt how to win even with the weapons they have to hand. It was not always so. There was a time when artists were *given* subjects to draw by writers, or at least had the subject warmly suggested to them by a gang of writers. That is why so many cartoons of before 1900 have dialogue. That is, two characters addressing each other, and *both speaking*. I don't think anyone has drawn a cartoon anywhere for more than fifty years in which more than one person speaks, but once upon a time it was considered quite all right for the characters in a drawing to have quite a little chat together, plus appropriate stage directions.

One old cartoon, not in this book, shows an elderly wife suspiciously holding up a ticket she's found on her husband's jacket. 'What's this, then?' 'Ah,' says the husband, improvising rapidly to conceal the fact that he's been to the pawnshop with it, 'I dropped in to the village dance at the weekend, and it was that hot I had to take my coat off. That's the cloakroom ticket for it.' Pause. 'There's a ticket on your trousers as well.'

That's all in one cartoon. It's more like a short story. In fact, it *is* a story, a writer's idea, and I have often found that you can *tell* someone a Victorian cartoon, and get a laugh for it, in a way you couldn't possibly with a modern cartoon. As if to compensate for having a tiny one-act play imposed on them, cartoonists would go to town on the background detail, fulfilling the artistic bit by lavishing attention on furniture, clothes, accessories, etc, in a way very few modern artists do, with the notable exception of Heath. During my time at *Punch* the library was occupied for a while by some very earnest researchers who spent hours poring over old cartoons. They turned out to be the designers for *Upstairs Downstairs*. God help the designer who had to rely on modern cartoons.

Well, the cartoonist seems to have got his freedom round about the time the women were getting the vote, and the cartoon became less a lovely drawing with story bolted on, more an integral piece. In other words, the picture started working more as a picture. The captions grew smaller, Phil May made it all right to have little background, and uncluttered pictures, until finally you got cartoons *with nobody speaking in them*. Who did it first, I don't know, but I suspect H M Bateman was well up with the first. Whether with long strip cartoons (like The Boy Who Breathed on the Glass at the British Museum, or the one-note orchestral player) or with his famous 'The Man Who' formula, Bateman made his drawings move – the joke jumps out at you, but it never becomes detached. You couldn't really *tell* a Bateman joke. It has become an integral part of the drawing – the way the colonel swells up with anger or the little man shrinks is inseparable from the way it's drawn.

And yet the cartoon with no caption has never become the norm. Cartoonists do like to have at least one person speaking, as otherwise they find themselves doing silent film gags. Max, the strange creature invented by Giovanetti, was a sort of Tom and Jerry figure. There are two cartoons in this book which have no caption, only silent movement. One, by Eric Burgin, shows a hand appearing from inside a gondola and sawing off the end on which the gondolier is standing, singing. The other, by André François, shows a husband afflicted by a nagging wife about to cut through the wire to his deaf aid. They are both pure silent movie gags. Actually, they are both the same gag, which shows where doing without words leads you.

And it's strange how often words do crop up in apparently captionless gags. Larry is alone among modern cartoonists in doing without captions; he also is alone in having so much writing *inside* his drawings, whether on signs, advertisements or the side of statues. Other cartoonists start to succumb to the temptation to put extra writing in, like Merrily Harpur or Handelsman in his Freaky Fables. I once did a strip feature in *Punch*, called 'Farming With Mark', based on the news that Mark Phillips was going to do an agricultural course and then become a farmer, and Ken Taylor did the drawings for my words. To begin with, his drawings were sober and admirable. Gradually, he introduced little handwritten jokes of his own. Finally, he was outwriting me in the ratio of 10 to 1, and I was forced to kill the strip out of sheer mortification.

Still, at least I have been asked to write the introduction to this book, a job which could well have been given to a cartoonist, at which point their victory over the writers would have been complete. I have had nothing to do with the selection of cartoons in this book, but all the ones I had hoped to see (the Bill Tidy polar bear joke, the Thomas Derrick 'Anything in the paper, darling?') are in here, and a lot I didn't know about as well. It's the variety that amazes me, from the elegance of Anton to the dowdiness of Sprod, from the modern look of Fougasse to the more old-fashioned look of Brockbank twenty years later, from ffolkes's magic line to Larry's equally personal chunky sweater look, from…

Well, what's the use. I entered the rich world of *Punch's* cartoons thirty years ago through R E Williams's *A Century of Punch*. It was a heady experience. I haven't seen a cartoon book since then quite like it. Now I have.

Index of Cartoonists

"Mmm, I just love to run my fingers through a man's wallet."

FURTHER ILLUSTRATION OF THE MINING DISTRICTS.

First Polite Native. "WHO'S 'IM, BILL?"
Second ditto. "A STRANGER!"
First ditto. "'EAVE 'ARF A BRICK AT 'IM."

1

How to Kill a Man in Six Efforts By RONALD SEARLE

1. Love

2. Indifference

3. Jealousy

4. Poison

5. Undernourishment

KOSIKOT

5. Strength

"Actually, they import the mechanism from the Swiss – but the concept is typically Haitian."

"Norman spent a lot of time down on the quay, watching the fishermen mending their nets. Until one day, they presented him with this lovely jersey."

"Right, the scene is set … release the mosquitoes, Bernard."

"Hey, guys! It's Yuppy!"

"It's clues we're looking for, constable."

"... AND ALFRED AND I *INSIST* ON HAVING OUR REVENGE NEXT WEEK."

First Cock Sparrow. "WHAT A MIWACKULOUS TYE, FWANK. HOW THE DOOSI DO YOU MANAGE IT?"
Second Cock Sparrow. "YAS. I FANCY IT IS RATHER GRAND; BUT THEN, YOU SEE, I GIVE THE WHOLE OF MY MIND TO IT!"

"YOU'LL BE WELL LOOKED AFTER NOW, OLD MAN; HERE COMES THE DISTRICT NURSE."

"You wife's on the phone —
a blue-tit's gone into the nesting-box."

8

Young Sister. "I SHOULD SO LIKE TO GO TO A PARTY, MA."

Mamma. "MY DEAR, DON'T BE RIDICULOUS. AS I HAVE TOLD YOU BEFORE (I AM SURE A HUNDRED AND FIFTY TIMES), THAT UNTIL FLORA IS MARRIED, IT IS UTTERLY IMPOSSIBLE FOR YOU TO GO OUT; SO DO NOT ALLUDE TO THE SUBJECT AGAIN, I BEG."

"They seek him here – they seek him there!"

"I've just got to the bottom of my 'in' tray, and look what I've found—a memo dated March 21st, 1947, giving me a month's notice."

ALCOHOFFNUNG

13

ZOOLOGY:

Railway Porter (to Old Lady travelling with a Menagerie of Pets). "'STATION MASTER SAY, MUM, AS CÁTS IS 'DOGS,' AND RABBITS IS 'DOGS,' AND SO'S PARROTS; BUT THIS ERE 'TORTIS' IS A INSECT, SO THERE AIN'T NO CHARGE FOR IT!'"

*"Well, gentlemen, we've got a stunning new logo and a marvellous publicity campaign ready.
We just need to come up with a product."*

"THE MUSIC OF THE FUTURE"!

Mamma (to her Daughter, who had just entered). "MABEL, DEAR, COME AND SIT WITH ME. WE'VE HAD ENOUGH WAGNER FOR THIS MORNING. I'M GETTING A LITTLE TIRED OF IT."

Mabel. "M'A, DEAR, I HAVEN'T BEEN TOUCHING THE PIANO. IT'S NURSE AND BABY!"

"That's an excellent suggestion, Miss Triggs. Perhaps one of the men here would like to make it."

OUR COUNTRYMEN ABROAD.

SKETCH OF A BENCH ON THE BOULEVARDS, OCCUPIED BY FOUR ENGLISH PEOPLE WHO ONLY KNOW EACH OTHER BY SIGHT.

Benevolent Old Gentleman. "Now then, little boy. What do you mean by bullying that little girl? Don't you know it's very cruel?"

Rude Little Boy. "Garn! wot's the trouble? She's my Sweetheart!"

Fussy Old Lady. "Now *don't* forget, Conductor. I *want the* Bank *of* England."
Conductor. "All right, Mum." (*Aside.*) "She *don't* want much, do she, Mate!"

"ARE YOU COMIN' 'OME?"
"I'LL DO ELLYTHIK YOU *LIKE* IN REASOL, M'RIA—(*hic*)—BUR I *WON'T* COME 'OME."

"...'I remind you of who?' I said.
And then I knocked the blighter down."

"You're noisy for a cat."

"No, no, you're not disturbing us. We were just horsing around listening to Webern, discussing Wittgenstein, and stuff like that."

"A coupon for your thoughts, dear."

FOGGY WEATHER.

"Has Mr. Smith been here?"   "Yes; he was here about an hour ago."
"Was I with him?"

21

Fond and resourceful Mother. "It's baby's birthday to-morrow. He's too young to invite children, so I'm having fifteen people in to play bridge."

NORMAN MANSBRIDGE

"Strange to think a whole generation has grown up knowing nothing of matching accessories."

EXPERIENTIA DOCET.

Elder of Fourteen. "WHERE'S BABY, MADGE?"   *Madge.* "IN THE OTHER ROOM, I THINK, EMILY."
Elder of Fourteen. "GO DIRECTLY, AND SEE WHAT SHE'S DOING, AND TELL HER SHE MUSTN'T!"

THRIFT.

Peebles Body (to Townsman who was supposed to be in London on a visit). " E—EH, MAC! YE'RE SUNE HAME AGAIN ! "

Mac. " E—EH, IT'S JUST A RUINOUS PLACE, THAT ! MUN, A HAD NA' BEEN THE-ERRE ABUNE TWA HOOURS WHEN—*BANG*—WENT *SAXPENCE ! ! !* "

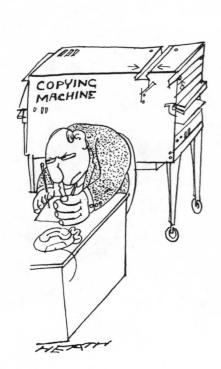

"Sorry, madam — the chef says he cannot reveal his sauces."

"I sometimes wonder if sponsorship isn't getting a little out of hand."

"IT WAS WHAT I CALL *CLASSIC* MUSIC, IF YOU KNOW WHAT I MEAN—NOT *JAZZ*."

The Vicar. "YOU SUSPECT HASHISH? BUT, GOOD HEAVENS, MAN, LOOK AT MY COLLAR!"

Zealous Customs. "YESS, YESS—PLENTY TIME. I SEARCH YOU UNDER THE COLLAR IN A MINUTE."

THE NEW ACT AGAIN. DIFFERENT POINTS OF VIEW.

Magistrate. "You are charged with having been drunk when in charge of a Child under the age of Seven Years."
Prisoner. "Please, your Worship, she was a-takin' me 'ome."

"The Old Man insisted I should begin as he did—with a paper round."

OFFICIALS by GERALD SCARFE

A Top Official at Work

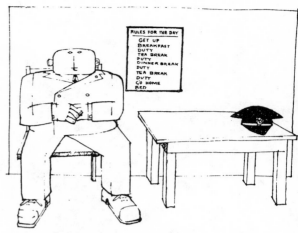

An Off-Duty Official at Home

"No! If I let you do it,
they'll all want to do it."

An Official Thinking up a Swift and Cutting Reply
to a Tentative Inquiry

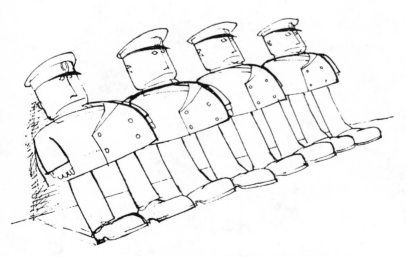

Off-Duty Officials Stacked for Immediate Use

"Sometimes I rather wish we hadn't expanded into a quintet."

"I don't know who he is—the children brought him back from their evacuation village."

"Charlie Jackson's daughter only charges four pounds an hour for tuition."

Batsman (in danger of being caught by small brother). "DROP IT, 'ERBERT—OR 'OME YOU GO!"

NEW CRICKETING DRESSES, TO PROTECT ALL ENGLAND AGAINST THE PRESENT SWIFT BOWLING

"If she doesn't make it as a ballet dancer, she wants to be a dentist."

TELEPHONIC COMMUNICATION.

Husband (off to Paris). "DON'T CRY, DARLING. IT'S *TOO* SAD TO LEAVE YOU, I *KNOW!* BUT YOU CAN TALK TO ME THERE JUST AS IF WE WERE TOGETHER—ONLY BE CAREFUL, AS IT'S EXPENSIVE!"

Wife. "IS IT, DARLING? HA-HA-HADN'T YOU BETTER LEAVE ME A FEW BLANK CHEQUES?"

AWARDING THE BISCUIT.

Dingy Bohemian. "I WANT A BATH OLIVER."
Immaculate Servitor. "MY NAME IS NOT OLIVER!"

THE STERNER SEX!

"HULLO, GERTY! YOU'VE GOT FRED'S HAT ON, AND HIS COVER COAT?"

"YES. DON'T YOU LIKE IT?"

"WELL — IT MAKES YOU LOOK LIKE A YOUNG MAN, YOU KNOW, AND THAT'S SO EFFEMINATE!"

"Hold those incoming calls, Larry. I'm teaching my new secretary the alphabet."

Eric Burgin

"Hello . . . Police? Well look here, there's someone here reading the Daily Bugle and my husband always reads the Daily Blah."

EXPERIENTIA DOCET?

Wife of Two Years' Standing. "OH YES! I'M SURE HE'S NOT SO FOND OF ME AS AT FIRST. HE'S AWAY SO MUCH, NEGLECTS ME DREADFULLY, AND HE'S SO CROSS WHEN HE COMES HOME. WHAT *SHALL* I DO?"
Widow. "FEED THE BRUTE!"

"What do you mean, you're not in the mood?"

Ken Pyne

*"Hello, folks, this is your Captain speaking. May I introduce my best friend, Boko?
Boko flies the aeroplane when I'm not feeling well."*

GOOD ADVERTISEMENT.

"I USED YOUR SOAP TWO YEARS AGO; SINCE THEN I HAVE USED
NO OTHER."

SATISFACTORY.

"Dining at Lady Laburnum's to-morrow?"   "Yaas."
"So am I."   "*So* Glad!"
"*So* Glad you're Glad!!"   "*SO* Glad you're Glad I'm Glad!!!"

"*I wonder if I could borrow a cupful of gin?*"

"Behold – an efficient information retrieval system, with on-line access to stored detail…"

Girl (to young man who has asked for a second cherry in his cocktail). "WHAT'S THE GREAT IDEA, TONY?"
Tony. "FAMILY MEDICAL ADVISER INSISTS I MUST EAT MORE FRUIT."

THE SLIMMING CRAZE.

Doctor. "AND DO YOU DRINK AT MEALS?"
Patient. "DON'T BE SILLY, DOCTOR. WHY, I DON'T EVEN *EAT* AT MEALS."

ALL THE DIFFERENCE!

Haberdasher (to Assistant who has had the "swop"). "WHY HAS THAT LADY GONE WITHOUT BUYING?"

Assistant. "WE HAVEN'T GOT WHAT SHE WANTS."

Haberdasher. "I'LL SOON LET YOU KNOW, MISS, THAT I KEEP YOU TO SELL WHAT I'VE GOT, AND NOT WHAT PEOPLE WANT!"

Dear Old Lady (very much up from the country, at the doors of London emporium). "MAY I COME IN?"

"Boy! What a party!"

"I think it's cruel the way they keep them cooped up in those little cages."

"Well, I'll marry you if you insist—but who do you suppose you're speaking to?"

Old Lady (describing a cycling accident). "'E 'ELPED ME HUP, AN' BRUSHED THE DUST ORF ON ME, AN' PUT FIVE SHILLIN' IN MY 'AND, AN' SO I SAYS, 'WELL, SIR, I'M SURE YOU'RE *HACTIN'* LIKE A GENTLEMAN,' I SAYS, 'THOUGH I DON'T SUPPOSE YOU ARE ONE,' I SAYS."

"They don't make frames like that nowadays."

"Go and see what's bothering him. He doesn't usually howl for nothing."

First Player. "HOW OUGHT WE TO DIVIDE? I'M PRETTY FEEBLE"
Second Ditto. "I EXPECT YOU'RE A LOT BETTER THAN I AM"
Third Ditto. "I'M HOPELESSLY ROTTEN"
Fourth Ditto (ignoring the conventions). "I'M RATHER HOT STUFF. NOW LET'S START OVER AGAIN"

Father. "Now, look here, you girls—when you grow up one of you must be able to speak French, and the other German."
Brenda. "All right, Dad; and Muriel had better learn German, because she can gargle best."

"I see the Hitachi deal fell through."

HUSBANDING—HIS RESOURCES.

Felix. "HEAD BAD TO-NIGHT, DARLING?"   *Beatrice.* "IT IS RATHER, DEAR."
Felix (mentally reviewing his accomplishments). "SHALL I—SMOKE A LITTLE TO YOU, DARLING?"

"You should have consulted the committee before you accepted the Snugfit Truss sponsorship, Major."

THE BRITISH CHARACTER
TENDENCY TO KEEP OUT OF FOREIGN POLITICS

SCENE—A Suburban Drawing-room. A Lady Collector for a Home for Incurable Children has just left.

Phyllis (aged three, the youngest of a large family, mostly boys). "WHAT DID THE LADY WANT, MOTHER?"

Mother. "SHE WAS BEGGING FOR POOR CHILDREN, DEAR."

Phyllis. "AND DID YOU GIVE HER THE BOYS?"

"He's a glutton for work—that's as close as he ever gets to a holiday."

"FINE ART," 1869.

Rural Connoisseur. "HE'S A P'INTIN' TWO PICTUR'S AT ONCE, D' YER SEE? 'BLEST IF I DON'T LIKE THAT THERE LITTLE 'UN AS HE'S GOT HIS THUMB THROUGH, THE BEST!"

"I DID ENJOY THAT. ISN'T IT MARVELLOUS HOW WE BOTH LOATHE THE SAME PEOPLE?"

"Best cigarette of the day, I always think…"

"It's a new kind of bomb, darling, for the benefit of mankind."

"Well, this certainly buggers our plan to conquer the Universe."

"No, I'm sorry—if I let **you** keep your underpants on, I'd have to let **everyone** keep their underpants on."

"My wife and I are thinking of going to Gaul."

ASSURANCE.

Fougasse

"GOOD MORNING. I WANT TO TAKE OUT AN INSURANCE POLICY.

I WANT TO INSURE AGAINST EVERY RISK THAT CAN BE INCLUDED IN THE POLICY—

AND, OF COURSE, AGAINST THE RISK OF ANYTHING HAPPENING THAT ISN'T MENTIONED IN THE POLICY—

AS ALSO AGAINST THE RISK OF FORGETTING TO RENEW THE POLICY—

AND, NATURALLY, AGAINST THE RISK OF NOT GETTING ALL THAT I CLAIM UNDER THE POLICY—

AS WELL AS AGAINST THE RISK OF LITIGATION WITH THE COMPANY OVER THE POLICY.

I WANT TO INSURE AGAINST THE RISK OF THE COMPANY GOING BUST AND NOT BEING ABLE TO CARRY OUT THE POLICY—

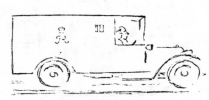

AND, ON THE OTHER HAND, AGAINST THE RISK OF GOING BUST MYSELF AND NOT BEING ABLE TO PAY THE PREMIUMS REQUIRED BY THE POLICY—

AND, FINALLY, AGAINST THE RISK OF NOT BEING ABLE TO GET THE POLICY AT ALL."

"Does it tick?"

"Well, well! Remember that? My pedestal!"

Visitor (at private hospital). "CAN I SEE LIEUTENANT BARKER, PLEASE?"

Matron. "WE DO NOT ALLOW ORDINARY VISITING. MAY I ASK IF YOU'RE A RELATIVE?"

Visitor (boldly). "OH, YES! I'M HIS SISTER."

Matron. "DEAR ME! I'M VERY GLAD TO MEET YOU. *I'M HIS MOTHER.*"

"*Would you change your name to Chippendale by deed poll, Mr. Hodges?—I have a sudden twinge of conscience.*"

"*Bloody hell, Jeanette, I thought you'd cancelled the Jehovah's Witnesses.*"

"Suddenly Fiona screamed at him like a scalded cat."

"Personally, Sergeant, I'd say suicide – but I think we're going to need a psychiatrist's report."

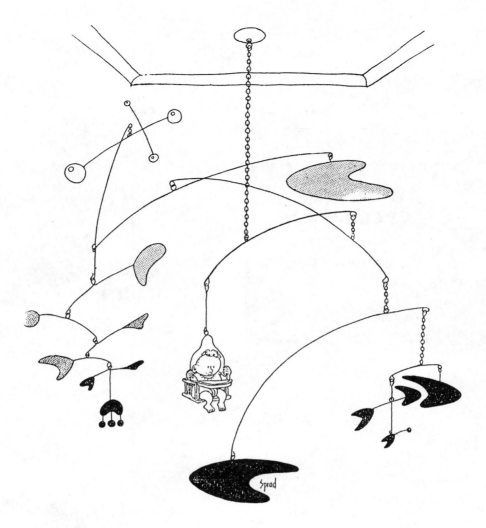

Excited Old Lady (as express thunders through station). "OH, PORTER, DOESN'T THAT TRAIN STOP HERE?"
Patient Porter. "NO, LIDY; IT DON'T EVEN HESITATE."

"How many more times, Miss Graham—not harassment, **har**assment!"

"They said, 'You'll never succeed in that parish.' They said, 'You'll never make an impression on that tight-lipped bunch of Puritans.' They said, 'You'll never find the key to the wine cupboard.' Well, two out of three 'aint bad."

"I CAN'T COME OUT YET, DEAR; I'M WASHING THE BABY."

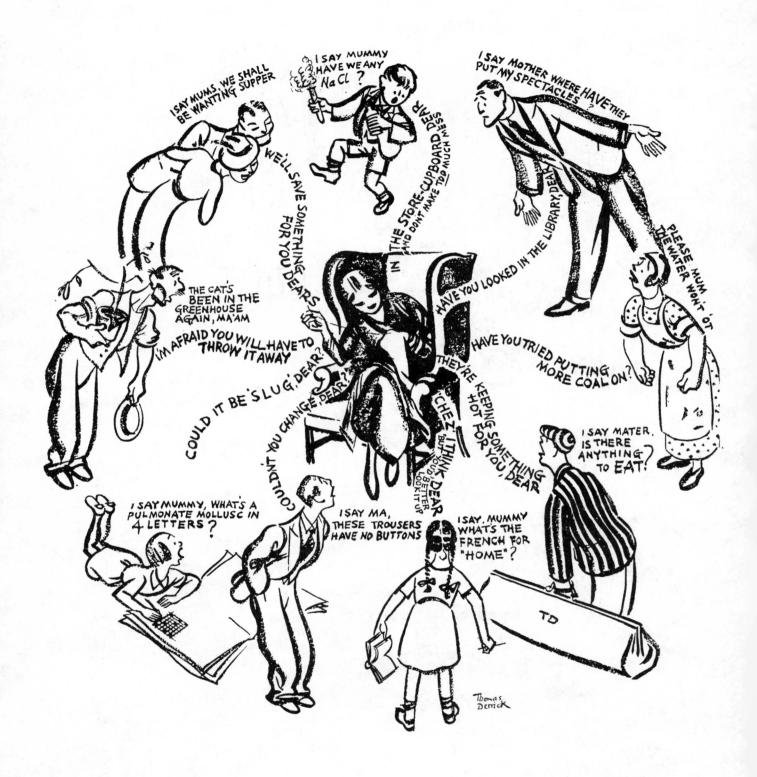

MOTHER

"They say most accidents happen in the home."

HER FIRST VISIT TO A POLICE-COURT.

Old Lady. "WHAT A VILLAINOUS-LOOKING MAN THE PRISONER IS!"
Friend. "HUSH! THAT'S NOT THE PRISONER. THAT'S THE MAGISTRATE!"

Peggy. "WAS THAT P'LICEMAN EVER A LITTLE BABY, MOTHER?"
Mother. "WHY, YES, DEAR."
Peggy (thoughtfully). "I DON'T B'LIEVE I'VE EVER SEEN A BABY P'LICEMAN!"

FIRST NIGHT OF AN UNAPPRECIATED MELODRAMA.

He. "ARE WE ALONE?"
Voice from the Gallery. "NO, GUV'NOR; BUT YOU WILL BE TO-MORROW NIGHT."

"He's wonderful with children…"

THE SOUFFLÉ

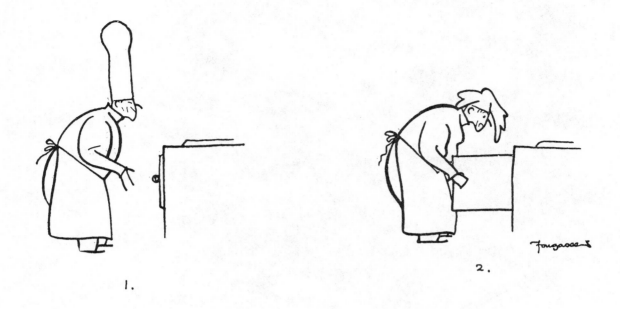

1.

2.

Voice from upper regions. "DEARIE, IF YOU CAN'T KEEP BABY QUIET, WHY NOT GIVE HIM SOMETHING TO PLAY WITH?"

The Vicar. "Now, children, what is a false doctrine?" Inspired Maiden. "Please, Sir, bad medicine."

McLACHLAN

CHANGE OF OCCUPATION.

Vicar's Wife (sympathisingly). "NOW THAT YOU CAN'T GET ABOUT, AND ARE NOT ABLE TO READ, HOW DO YOU MANAGE TO OCCUPY THE TIME?"

Old Man. "WELL, MUM, SOMETIMES I SITS AND THINKS; AND THEN AGAIN I JUST SITS."

"You're always just popping down to the water hole."

"Remember the good old days when we could grind our own teeth?"

Polite Rustic. "Oh! Arter yeaou, Mum."

"I still reckon we should 'ave been the 8.35 to the City!"

Affectionate Husband. "COME, POLLY—IF I AM A LITTLE IRRITABLE, IT'S OVER IN A MINUTE!!"

"Oh God no! Not the '23!"

"They say he was
a child prodigy."

First Elegant Creature. " A—Don't you Dance, Charles ? "
Second ditto, ditto. " A—No—Not at Pwesent ! I always let the Girls look, and long for me first ! "

"Well, that rules out a coalition."

"Just because it's in his own hand, Mrs Figmarsh, doesn't automatically make it a legal will."

SIGNING OFF

Yours in haste ...

Yours faithfully

Ever yours

Your loving son ...

Cordially yours

Yours sincerely

Your most obedient servant

Ronald Searle

Yours till the cows come home ..

"That reminds me, dear—did you remember the sandwiches?"

"Could you make it just a bit more compassionate and caring?"

"I'm terribly sorry you've had such a wretched cold, Lady Sheba."
"Yes, it's that new maid of mine. She WILL put my jewellery on me without taking the chill off."

"THEY TELL ME YOU 'RE WORKIN' HARD NIGHT AND DAY SINCE YOU WERE UP BEFORE THE MAGISTRATE FOR PUSHIN' YOUR HUSBAND ABOUT, MRS. ROBINSON."

"YES. THE MAGISTRATE SAID IF I CAME BEFORE HIM AGAIN HE'D FINE ME FORTY SHILLINGS."

"AND SO YOU 'RE WORKIN' HARD TO KEEP OUT OF MISCHIEF?"

"WHAT?—I 'M WORKIN' HARD TO SAVE UP THE FINE."

"It wouldn't really be ethical for the board to sanction me a substantial increase. I'm therefore having to take it under the table."

"I just live for the day when we catch those Roman bastards at it, that's all."

"The dog's being impossible again."

"D' YOU MIND SWITCHING OFF, SIR? SHE'S GAININ' ON ME."

THE FIRST SCRATCH—

AND THE LAST.

85

"Personally, I find the continued lack of confidence in sterling very disturbing."

"JUST RUN 'OME AN' FETCH ME MY SMALL 'AMMER, ALBERT."

.thelwell.

Nurse (to fond mother of celebrated musical prodigy). "PLEASE, MUM, IS MASTER WILLY TO 'AVE 'IS MORNING SLEEP, OR GO ON WIV 'IS SIXTEENTH SYMPHERNY?"

"I've always been a one-man woman, Gerald, and for
the past four years it hasn't been you."

"You'll have to excuse Dorothy — it's that time of the month."

". . . and this is my wife's little den."

"First the good news. His temperature has gone down."

Employer. "Isn't it rather strange that your grandfather should be seriously ill every time there's a big football match on?"
Office Boy. "Yessir. I sometimes wonder if he's shammin.'"

Urchin (to friend who has gone in). "B-I-I-LL! lend us yer skates; you ain't using 'em!"

MORE COMPLIMENTARY THAN IT SEEMS.

Papa (concluding the fascinating Tale). "'AND HE WAS TURNED INTO A BEAUTIFUL PRINCE, AND MARRIED BEAUTY'"!
Minnie (after a pause). "PAPA, WERE *YOU* A BEAST BEFORE YOU MARRIED MAMMA?"

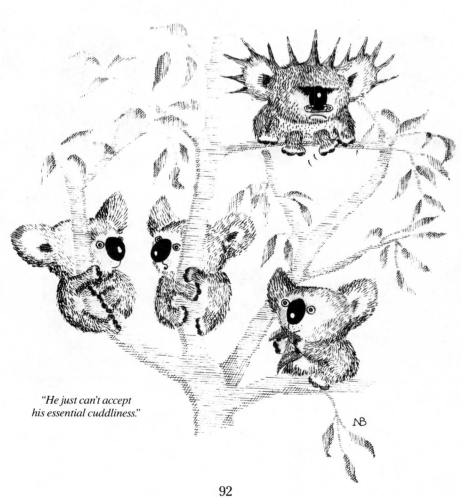

"He just can't accept his essential cuddliness."

*"Well, that's enough about me, Father—what have you
been up to lately?"*

Newly-Affianced Young Lady (who is never going to forget the dance she has just had). "CAN YOU TELL ME THE NAME OF THAT
LOVELY TUNE YOU JUST PLAYED?"
Member of the Orchestra. "CERTAINLY. IT'S CALLED 'I *DO* LIKE MY LITTLE DROP OF BEER'"

Hospital Patient (one of large family in poor district, given a glass of milk). "How far down can I drink?"

Diminutive "Nipper." "'ERE, THIS AIN'T ARF ALL RIGHT! NEX TIME I WANTS ARF A PINT, I SHALL 'AVE TO SEND FATHER!"

"Last time, failed to keep appointment, caused you considerable inconvenience, gave no excuse or apology."

TRUE HUMILITY.

Right Reverend Host. "I'm afraid you've got a bad egg, Mr. Jones!"
The Curate. "Oh no, my Lord, I assure you! Parts of it are excellent!"

'MARK MY WORDS, MR. GOLDERSTEIN
THIS IS GOING TO REVOLUTIONISE THE ART
OF VENTRILOQUISM.'

"Oh no, the place has been ransacked!"

"Adrian doesn't *do* anything –
he's creative."

First Domestic Servant (referring to her neighbour's master). "WHAT'S YOUR BIT O' TROUBLE'S 'USBAND?"
Second Ditto. "'IM! OH, 'E'S SOMETHIN' IN THE CITY, BUT 'E AIN'T NOTHIN' AT 'OME."

*"The practice of astrology took a major step toward achieving
redibility today when, as predicted, everyone born under the sign
of Scorpio was run over by an egg lorry."*

99

"*What's up with you lately, old chap—is it some girl?*"

"*See here, Ritterhaus, I want TV commercials that will give people headaches and upset-stomachs.*"

"DID I REALLY UNDERSTAND YOU, MISS WILSON, TO USE THE EXPRESSION, 'A COSY NOOK,' IN CONNECTION WITH THE HOUSE YOU WISH ME TO DESIGN FOR YOU?"

"I'll take them!"

"Waiter, there's a fly in my soup."

A HOME TRUTH.

Host (sotto voce). "Is this the *best* Claret, Mary?"   *Mary (audibly).* "It's the best you've got, Sir!"

"What do you mean, I look very prosperous? I am very prosperous."

"Sorry, He doesn't do toasters."

"Something to do with the nationalization of railways, I expect."

"You have to admit,
he's adjusted extremely well
to the new technology."

Ken Pyne

"Would you mind if you passively smoked?"

"The pity is, after Goliath I'm afraid he never quite matched up to his original promise."

"WHERE ARE YOU OFF TO?"
"TO THE DOCTOR. I DON'T LIKE THE LOOK OF MY WIFE."
"I'LL COME WITH YOU. I HATE THE SIGHT OF MINE."

"WELL, JACK! HERE'S GOOD NEWS FROM HOME. WE'RE TO HAVE A MEDAL."
"THAT'S VERY KIND. MAYBE ONE OF THESE DAYS WE'LL HAVE A COAT TO STICK IT ON?"

"Yes, but is there any news of the iceberg?"

"*It's a little chilly, so I've put an extra dog on your bed.*"

CREMATION.

Nephew. "I HOPE YOU HAVEN'T BEEN WAITING LONG, UNCLE?"

Uncle. "ALL RIGHT, MY BOY. BEEN READING THE PAPER, AND HAD A PINCH—— BY THE BYE, IT'S QUEER FLAVOURED SNUFF IN THIS JAR OF YOURS, FRED."

Nephew (aghast). "SNUFF, UNCLE!—JAR! GOOD GRACIOUS!—THAT'S NOT SNUFF! THOSE ARE THE ASHES OF MY LANDLORD'S FIRST WIFE!"

"…and that's jazz!"

*"We like the plot, Miss Austen, but all this effing
and blinding will have to go."*

*"The big problem with your illness, Mr Hawkins,
is that nobody famous has caught it yet."*

FOND AND FOOLISH.

Edwin (suddenly, after a long pause). "DARLING!"   *Angelina.* "YES, DARLING!"
Edwin. "NOTHING, DARLING. ONLY *DARLING*, DARLING!"   [*Bilious Old Gentleman feels quite sick.*

111

Nervous Servant (to noble Duke). "GRACE, YOUR GROUSE?"

"THERE'S A MOOSE LOOSE!"
"ARE YOU ENGLISH OR SCOTS?"

THE BOY WHO BREATHED ON THE GLASS IN THE BRITISH MUSEUM.

AN ANTE-BELLUM TRAGEDY.

H.M. BATEMAN. 1916

A SECRET OF THE SEA.

Passenger. "Look here, Steward, if this is Coffee, I want Tea; but if this is Tea, then I wish for Coffee."

"There's usually four of us but Pestilence is running in the 3.30 at Uttoxeter."

Mr. Binks. "ONE OF MY ANCESTORS FELL AT WATERLOO."
Lady Clare. "AH? WHICH PLATFORM?"

*"You urgently need a holiday,
Mr Abthorpe –
Might I suggest Lourdes?"*

Doctor. "WHAT DID YOU OPERATE ON JONES FOR?"
Surgeon. "A HUNDRED POUNDS."
Doctor. "NO, I MEAN WHAT HAD HE GOT?"
Surgeon. "A HUNDRED POUNDS."

"The one in the grey suit is the author. The others are accountants."

"Our spells have never been the same since we got the bleedin' wok."

"It's a tree son...a tree."

"GARGE, YOU AND I BE COORTING NOW FOR NIGH ON TEN YEAR, IT'S 'BOUT TIME WE THOORT O' GETTING WED."
"AYE, LASS, BUT 'OO WOULD 'AVE US NOW?"

*"My agent said it was a remake of the 'Prisoner of Zenda'
but apparently it's a commercial for Rawlplugs."*

"How many more times must I tell you to sprawl properly, Lucius?"

Summer Number 1951

VOLUME CCXXI

"Your wife still on holiday, old man?"

A FRACTIOUS STEED.

"Actually, I collapsed while taking part in the East Grimpton Operatic Society's production of 'Faust'."

"Every day he changes into a computer programmer and makes for the city. Heaven knows what he gets up to."

" Don't stop him, darling ! It's his form of self-expression."

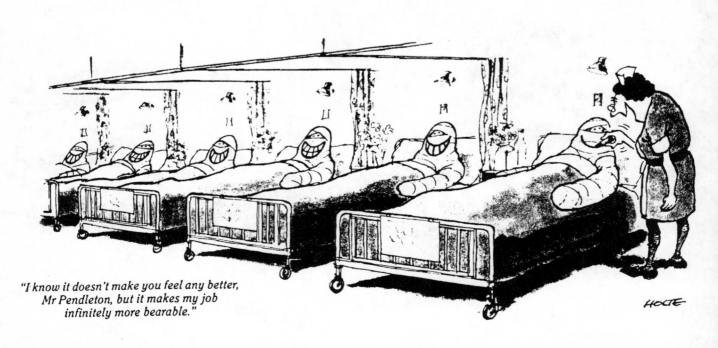

*"I know it doesn't make you feel any better,
Mr Pendleton, but it makes my job
infinitely more bearable."*

That dear old Mrs. Wilkinson (who can't always express exactly what she means to say, meeting Jones with the girl of his choice). "AND IS THIS YOUNG LADY YOUR FIASCO, MR. JONES?"

"I can't serve you."
"Well, fetch the bloke as can."

"I'm sorry, J.B., the Company feels that you have failed to live up to the desk."

"Here's your problem – the batteries are in upside-down."

ENTERTAINMENTS AT WHICH WE HAVE NEVER ASSISTED.

"Balancing the Books" at the Annual Dinner of the Society of Chartered Accountants.

"Yes?"

"Forget the crêpe suzette, Minchin — I'll have the rice pudding."

"Tell me more about this kleptomaniac tendency, Mrs. Henderson."

"A table for four incredibly obese, offensive,
yet extremely rich bastards!"

"I'm afraid he still hasn't quite mastered the new technology."

"Forgotten your key again, George?"

"And another thing—you'll have to stop him drawing all over the walls."

OUTRAGED INNOCENCE.

First Workman. "'E SAID 'E SAW ME 'URRY. 'E DIDN'T SEE ME 'URRY. 'E MUST HAVE SEEN 'URRY."

Second Workman (stung to the quick). "'E NEVER SAW ME 'URRY. I NEVER 'URRY."

"Now you're in big trouble. Here comes my solicitor."

Boy. "WELL, ALL I CAN SAY IS, MOTHER, IF THAT'S WHAT THEY DO AT UMBRIAN SCHOOLS I'M JOLLY GLAD I BELONG TO AN ENGLISH ONE."

"Then, of course, there'll be the usual search fee."

"Have you tried drink?"

The Lady. "WHAT WOULD YOUR MOTHER THINK IF SHE SAW YOU SMOKING?"
The Boy. "WHAT WOULD YOUR HUSBAND THINK IF HE SAW YOU SPEAKING TO A STRANGE MAN?"

FOR BETTER, FOR WORSE.

Mistress. "I'M SORRY YOU WANT TO LEAVE, ELLIS. ARE YOU GOING TO BETTER YOURSELF?"
Maid. "NO, M'M; I'M GOING TO GET MARRIED."

"He said they give him a headache when he takes them out."

"I said, we must have lunch some time."

"I think I saw an eyelid flicker."

"The insects are polythene too, of course."

"Net!"

COUNSEL CALLS THE JUDGE "MISTER."

Constable (to Motorist who has exceeded the speed limit). "AND I HAVE MY DOUBTS ABOUT THIS BEING YOUR FIRST OFFENCE. YOUR FACE SEEMS FAMILIAR TO ME."

"I just shook his hand and he was sick."

"Everything in this house is non-fattening. How come we're still fat?"

Wife. "LUMME! TO GET ANYTHINK AHT O' YOU'S LIKE TRYIN' TO OPEN A OYSTER WITH A BUS-TICKET."

"OF COURSE I REALISE THAT YOU FIND HER ATTRACTIVE, MY BOY, BUT DON'T FORGET THAT BEAUTY IS ONLY SKIN DEEP."

HEATH ROBINSON

THE FUSE

"Good heavens, Dorian – how dreadful!"

Mistress (hearing a crash). "WELL, COOK, WHAT IS IT NOW? TWO BASINS BROKEN!"
Cook. "YES'M. MARY BROKE THAT ONE, AND THIS 'ERE ONE JUST COME TO PIECES IN MY 'AND."

HOFFNUNG'S
MENAGERIE

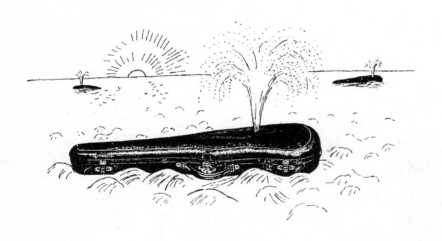

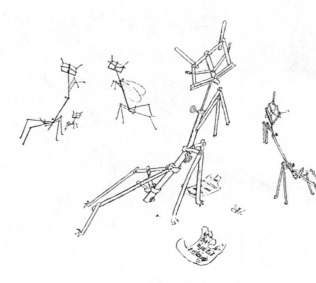

"Sorry to be the bearer of bad tidings, Thigben, but your retirement was a computer error."

"Don't give it a second thought—I'm always doing irreparable damage in other people's houses myself.

Customer. "THESE SHOES I BOUGHT FROM YOU ARE TOO FLIMSY TO WALK IN."
Manageress. "OUR ESTABLISHMENT, MADAM, DOES NOT PRETEND TO CATER FOR PEDESTRIANS."

"Look, I'm sorry you're so depressed, dear, but I've told you before never to ring me at the office!"

"That's Marcus in his prime—proud, arrogant and top of the heap, yet tenderness itself with his loved ones. I forget who the man is."

UNFORTUNATE POSITION OF SKATER WHEN ONLY PASSER-BY WAS A FASCIST.

Prudent Swain (*choosing valentine*). "PERHAPS YOU CAN HELP ME, MISS; WHAT I'M REALLY LOOKING FOR IS SOMETHING FRIGHTFULLY ARDENT YET DEFINITELY NON-COMMITTAL."

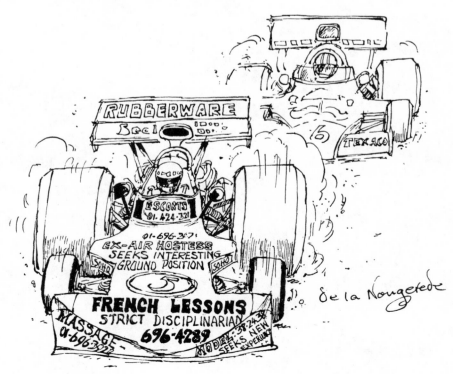

"I SOMETIMES THINK, SIR, IF I COULD HAVE MY LIFE OVER AGAIN I'D PART MY HAIR IN THE MIDDLE, SAME AS YOU."

"...A little more to the left."

" I KEEP THINKING IT'S TUESDAY."

BANX

*"What's the matter, dear?
Cat got your tongue?"*

SOUTHERN
FRUIT

TENNESSEE
JONES

smilby

"Same old story—boy meets boy."

"We say 'guilty', your honour –
guilty as a weasel in a hen-house."

THE EXTREME PENALTY.

She. "What do you think of his execution?"   *He.* "I'm in favour of it."

"I don't mind him. It's the people he brings into the house."

BEST EATEN BEFORE
16 B.C.

HOLTE

"GEORGE, HAVE YOU A SENSE OF HUMOUR?"
"I HOPE SO, DARLING. WHY?"
"BECAUSE THIS IS THE EXACT SPOT WHERE ERNEST AND I SWORE ETERNAL DEVOTION."

Employer. "Look at this letter from Messrs. Smith, beautifully typed."
Typist. "Um—and the grammar's excellent too."

"You may come in, Gover. Sir Henry has, I think, cast his last dart."

"Nothing I can do, I'm afraid. It's an occupational hazard."

THE MAN WHO PAID OFF HIS OVERDRAFT.

UNCLE TOM THE BACHELOR.

Fond Papa. "Do look, Emily! How *thoroughly* dear Tom is enjoying himself with those Kids!"

Doting Mamma. "Yes, *isn't* he! Dear little things! You see he has all the Pleasure of them, and none of the Trouble and Bother!"

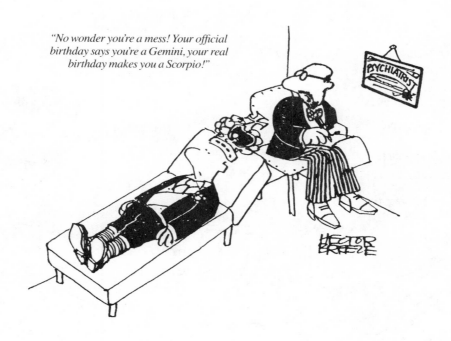

"No wonder you're a mess! Your official birthday says you're a Gemini, your real birthday makes you a Scorpio!"

" Between you and me, sir, we don't quite know where THAT line goes to."

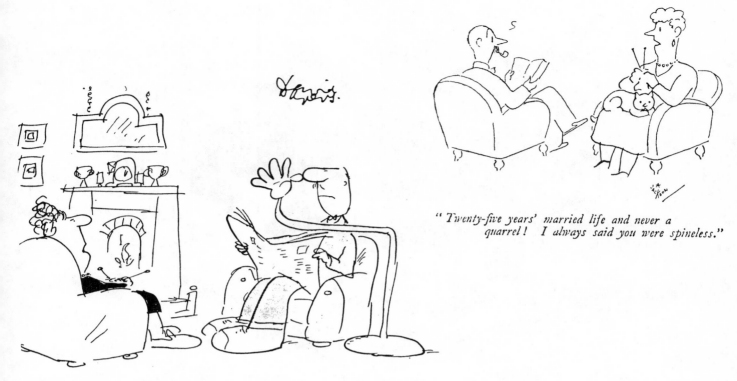

"Twenty-five years' married life and never a quarrel! I always said you were spineless."

"Why not admit it—you despise me."

THE BRITISH CHARACTER.
LOVE OF WRITING LETTERS TO *The Times.*

"Henderson, sell my mother."

"Fetch me the law for the rich, will you?"

IRISH ARCHITECTURE.

Angler (in Ireland). "HULLO, PAT, WHAT ARE YOU ABOUT NOW?"
Pat. "SHURE, I'M RAISIN' ME ROOF A BIT, YER HONOUR-R!!"

"At one time, we considered banning smoking altogether."

"Steward's enquiry? What steward's enquiry?"

"You will soon mug a tall dark stranger."

"We had to do something since McCartie doesn't work well with people."

"I think he's trying to tell us they're closing."

"THEY CAN'T *ALL* HAVE FORGOTTEN;
CARTWRIGHT MAJOR FOR ONE WROTE
DOWN THE DATE IN BLOOD."

"Of course, Margaret working is a great help. She buys all her own gin."

"Strewth, Norm – you look like you've just seen a ghost!"

*"Then he turned round
and poked his big
finger in my eye."*

"Too bad, gentlemen – I happen to be wearing my Swiss Army suit!"

"Oh, he won't bother with this lot. He only burns first editions."

"Good news! I found a bridge partner for your mum."

"Isn't that the fellow who paints miniatures?"

"Actually, I only need one way"

"How are things otherwise?"

"WOULD IT INTEREST YOU TO SEE MY SON'S REPORT?"
"NO."

"Your bath's ready, dear."

*"Why, Kilburn, how quaint! You want a rise
because you deserve one."*

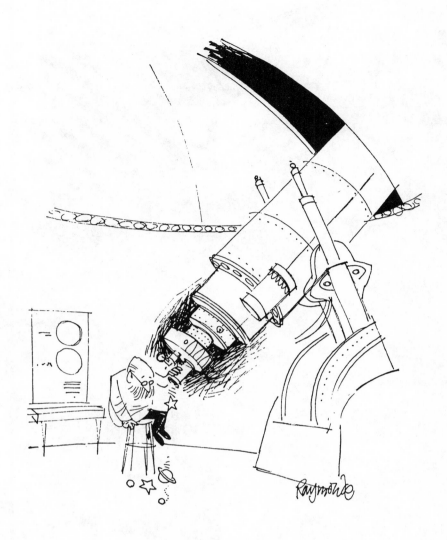

"I think I'm getting a chemistry set."

*"Why, Mr Willis! I'm glad to see you're improving
enough to sit up and fall over!"*

PRIMUM VIVERE, DEINDE PHILOSOPHARI.

"Is Florrie's engagement really off, then?"

"Oh, yes. Jack wanted her to give up gambling and smoking, and goodness knows what else."

(*Chorus.*) "How absurd!!"

SIGNATURES

"But I've said thank you."

"I understand they bought the place for a song."

"Hello, Sainsbury's?
Do you sell dog food
for very naughty puppies?
No? Well, I certainly
don't blame you.
Thank you, Sainsbury's,
and goodbye."

"Pigswill, yes, but great pigswill!"

"He's worried about getting old. He counted the first brown hairs among the pink this morning."

"We've been refused planning permission!"

SO LET US HAVE FAITH IN OUR LEADERS →

FORWARD!

"Oh, don't fuss, there'll be another one along in a minute."

"Of course, I've a profound respect for traditions, old boy—after all, without them, what have you got?"

The Architect Explains

ARNOLD ROTH

" . . . and, as a creative person, I feel it only right to assert my emotional self."

"It's no longer a matter of aesthetics—but one of economics."

"I let my buildings speak for me."

*"If people are mesmerised by the word 'Georgian,'
why should I disillusion them?"*

*"To me, it's more than a religious monument—it's
the expression of an ideal."*

"I merely assert modern man's desire to reassume his place in nature."

Man Decorating

By Larry

Working Man sitting on the steps of a big house in, say, Russell Square, smoking pipe. A mate passes by with plumbing tools, &c.

Man with tools. "HULLO, JIM! WOT ARE YER DOIN' 'ERE? CARETAKIN'?"

Man on steps. "NO. I'M THE HOWNER, 'ERE."

Man with tools. "'OW'S THAT?"

Man on steps. "WHY, I DID A BIT O' PLUMBING IN THE 'OUSE, AN' I TOOK THE PLACE IN PART PAYMENT FOR THE JOB."

"It's The Wild again."

"Your hearing-aid, you twisted, miserable old ratbag."

'You must have seen a lot of changes since you began as a teacher.'

"I thought I might stay in tonight and read my jacket."

Everybody who remembers the old days agrees that modern machinery has taken all the colour . . .

. . . out of country life.

"*I hate to do this, but I've just taken on a huge mortgage.*"

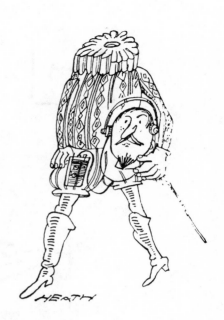

Ugly Coster. "'Oo are yer starin' at?"
The Other. "I ain't good at Natural 'Istory."

183

"Where's that waiter with our fish course?"

"Come on in…the water's horrible."

"…and when I give the word, Your Majesty, run like hell for the Batmobile."

"What's gone wrong, Fiona? We don't seem to dance cheek to cheek any more."

"Never mind me—get cracking on the reviewers."

THE BRITISH CHARACTER

IMPORTANCE OF NOT BEING INTELLECTUAL

'It says he's an egotistical, shallow, insincere little bore and if he's not careful he could end up with his own chat show!'

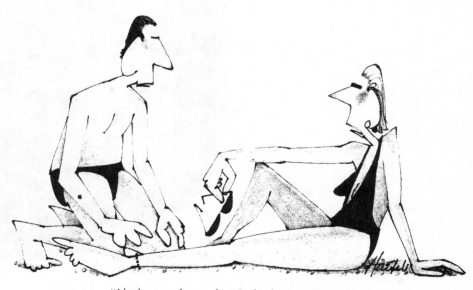

"I had you under my skin, Carlos, but now I'm peeling."

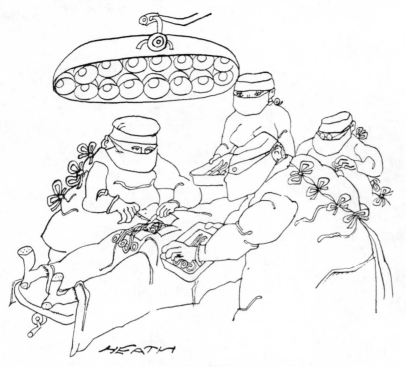

"He contains artificial flavouring, vegetable colouring, albumen, plus additives…"

"There…there it goes again, 'hi-ho, hi-ho'…"

*"Every week I tell him we don't sell the
Church Times or the Methodist Recorder…"*

"Some people just can't take those early post-retirement months!"

"Your car will be ready in a couple of weeks, sir. Our senior partner is personally handling the final series of road tests."

"I began by going back to nature and ended up by going to seed."

"I don't want your money – I want your easy-going charm, your wealth of knowledge, your talent to amuse..."

"And returned by one o'clock. I go to lunch then."

"Never mind what's wrong with 'im – just read the meter and go."

"Don't look now, but behind you I think life is beginning to imitate television commercials."

"It may be art but it's bloody poor welding."

"'Please excuse Arthur from all sports as he has a very bad cold.' You know that this sort of attitude cuts absolutely no ice with me, don't you, Potterton?"

"Oh God! What's Walter brought back this time?"

"No, m'sieur, on the whole the Spurs supporters behaved themselves quite well here in Belgium last week."

Young Husband. "I CAN'T STAND THIS SUSPENSE ANY LONGER. IT WILL KILL ME."
Doctor. "CALM YOURSELF, MY DEAR SIR. I'VE BROUGHT THOUSANDS OF BABIES INTO THE WORLD AND NEVER LOST A FATHER YET."

"Guess who's been made condom monitor?"

"Listen! There it is again—that persistent, dull knocking sound."

"The insurance money didn't amount to much then?"

"Sir Gawain said he was sorry he had slain the woman. Sir Bors then proposed a resolution opposing *the slaying of women*, which was passed. A very large knight rode in and challenged the entire company; this was tabled for a twelvemonth. There being no further business, we adjourned."

*"Don't worry, the wife won't be back from her macramé, or origami, or whatever
the hell she's studying these days."*

"Will ye tak' the paper?"
"Thanks. I don't care for reading in the train."
"Maybe. But will ye kindly cover yer knees wi' it? A 've nae wish to contemplate them."

"And now perhaps a quick word from Driver Firebrace, who is determined that the Yuletide mail shall get through on time . . ."

"A fine time to tell me now that your little girl is missing."

THE BEARD MOVEMENT.

Mr. Bristles. "THEN YOU REALLY THINK IT AN IMPROVEMENT, EH?"
Miss Spikes. "DECIDEDLY—IT HIDES SO MUCH MORE OF YOUR FACE."

"That Beryl Cook's got a lot to answer for."

Prize Idiot. "HOW EVER DO YOU MANAGE WITHOUT EXERCISE? IT TAKES ME ALL MY TIME TO KEEP FIT."
Worker. "FIT! FOR *WHAT*?"

"*. . . And if I'm really nice, he'll take me up in his helicopter.*"

BANX

"Two hundred billion people up here and I'm supposed to remember the usual?"

NECESSITY
NOT CHOICE
WIFE & CHILD

THE APOLOGIST.

"Yes, there's always a certain amount of disturbance as one actually goes _through_ the sound barrier."

"Here's the bastard now **and** he's carrying our Maude's bladder."

"Why can't we have what we had last year—leg?"

THE BRITISH CHARACTER.

"ADAPTABILITY TO FOREIGN CONDITIONS."

ILLUSTRATIONS OF HUMBUG.—Nº. I.

"'Tis true there is a slight difference in our ages, but with hearts that love, such considerations become frivolous. The world! Pshaw! Did you but love as I do, you would care but little for its opinion. Oh! say, beautiful being, will you be mine?"

"Solicitors can make a lot of money. Yes, if I were you I'd mug a solicitor."

A PERFECT WRETCH.

Wife. " Why, dear me, William ; how Time flies ! I declare we have been married Ten Years to-day !

Wretch. " Have we, love ? I am sure I thought it had been a great deal longer."

"*This is what comes of marrying a career woman.*"

smilby

"Let me sue! I'm a lawyer!"

"You had him worried that round. He thought he'd killed you."

"He's terribly shy. It was his turn to take off his shirt."

"Cancelled? . . . the Darts Match?"

Hostess. "Oh, so you sketch, do you?"   Artist Guest. "Yes."
Hostess. "But how nice! So much cheaper for you than photography."

"Sandy Gall…News at Ten…Canta Pero.."

"I went on an ego trip once and nobody noticed."

" Rabbit, Sir ? "

"I really wanted to go to Cambridge."

"WELL, MY DEAR, I HAD HIM HALVED AND STUFFED. I THINK HE MAKES A BEAUTIFUL PAIR."

"I knew this was coming. I've seen this many times."

"Be ever mindful, Farson, that not only must justice be done – it must be paid to be done."

"I KNOW, MY DEAR, BUT PENDLETON IS SO INDISPENSABLE, AND HE REFUSES TO BE SEPARATED FROM HIS TWIN."

"OH, YES, I'D ALWAYS GIVE UP MY SEAT TO A LADY—IF ONE EVER SUCCEEDED IN FIGHTING HER WAY IN."

"Let's face it, everything to do with it has been a cock-up from the word go."

"That you, dear?"

"Now, if we're going to put this over properly, you'll have to learn German."

"No – stupid boy! Exclamation mark! Doesn't that pratt
Bairnswater teach you anything?"

"OF COURSE, THERE'S ONE THING THAT NO FOREIGNER WILL EVER UNDERSTAND, AND THAT'S
OUR ENTHUSIASM FOR CRICKET."

"I'm going to call it football!"

THE BRITISH CHARACTER

ABILITY TO BE RUTHLESS

"HULLO!——YES?!——YES?!!—

YES?!!!——WHO IS IT?!!!!—

WHO IS IT?!!!!!—

OH . . . IT'S YOU . . .

MY DEAR, HOW PERFECTLY DELIGHTFUL
TO HEAR YOUR VOICE!!!"

Q. E. D.

"WHAT'S UP WI' SAL?"   "AIN'T YER ERD? SHE'S MARRIED AGIN!"

"We made it! We made it! We're on the Endangered Species list!"

"They say their lives are in danger if they go back!"

"Just think, my dear … if this is what man is capable of achieving in the seventeenth century, imagine what he'll be capable of by the twentieth!"

" There goes a car with exactly the same number as ours."

"He has your greed, darling."

Schoolmistress. "AND AM I TO GIVE THE CHILD RELIGIOUS INSTRUCTION?"
Mother. "I DON'T CARE WOT YER DO SO LONG AS YER DON'T BASH 'ER ABAHT THE 'EAD."

"*He's utterly convinced that he's being exiled to St. **Helen's**, poor devil!*"

"I think we're all agreed then – Blend 79 just about has it all."

"Mr McGregor's got a Flymo!"

DELIGHTS OF A HOTEL LOUNGE.

"AND WHAT WAS IT YOU SAID YOU WERE SUFFERING FROM?"

"I'm none too proud of that one. He thought I was taking his picture."

Pamela. "How's your wife, Peter?"
Peter. "She died last Tuesday."
Pamela. "Are you sorry?"
Peter. "Sorry? Of course I'm sorry. I *liked* the woman."

Bump
Bump
Bump

"Well, Piglet, that's the last we'll see of his ruddy computer."

THE ART OF BIDDING.

SOME DO IT BY THE RAISING
OF AN EYEBROW,

SOME BY A SLIGHT INCLINA-
TION OF THE HEAD,

SOME WITH A WINK,

SOME BY ADJUSTING THEIR TIE,

SOME BY ELEVATING THE
CATALOGUE—

OR A FOREFINGER,

SOME BY THE REMOVAL OF
THEIR SPECTACLES,

ANOTHER BY REPLACING
THEM,

BUT THE HEATHEN—HE DOES
IT BY WORD OF MOUTH.

"To be honest, Miriam, I'd never realised I was this important."